Everyday Mathematics®

Activity Sheets and Home Links

Everyday Mathematics®

Activity Sheets and Home Links

The University of Chicago
School Mathematics Project

 Wright Group

The McGraw·Hill Companies

UCSMP Elementary Materials Component

Max Bell, Director

Authors

Jean Bell, UCSMP
Max Bell, UCSMP
Dorothy Freedman,
    formerly of The University of Chicago Laboratory Schools
Nancy Guile Goodsell (First Edition)
Nancy Hanvey,
    formerly of Kozminski School, Chicago
Kate Morrison,
    formerly of The University of Chicago Laboratory Schools

Photo Credits

Cover: Bill Burlingham/Photography
Photo Collage: Herman Adler Design Group

Wright Group

Send all inquiries to:
Wright Group/McGraw-Hill
P.O. Box 812960
Chicago, IL 60681

ISBN 1-57039-943-3

17 18 PO 09 08 07 06

The **McGraw-Hill** Companies

Activity Sheets

Activity Sheets (cont.)

Coins

Activity
Sheet
1

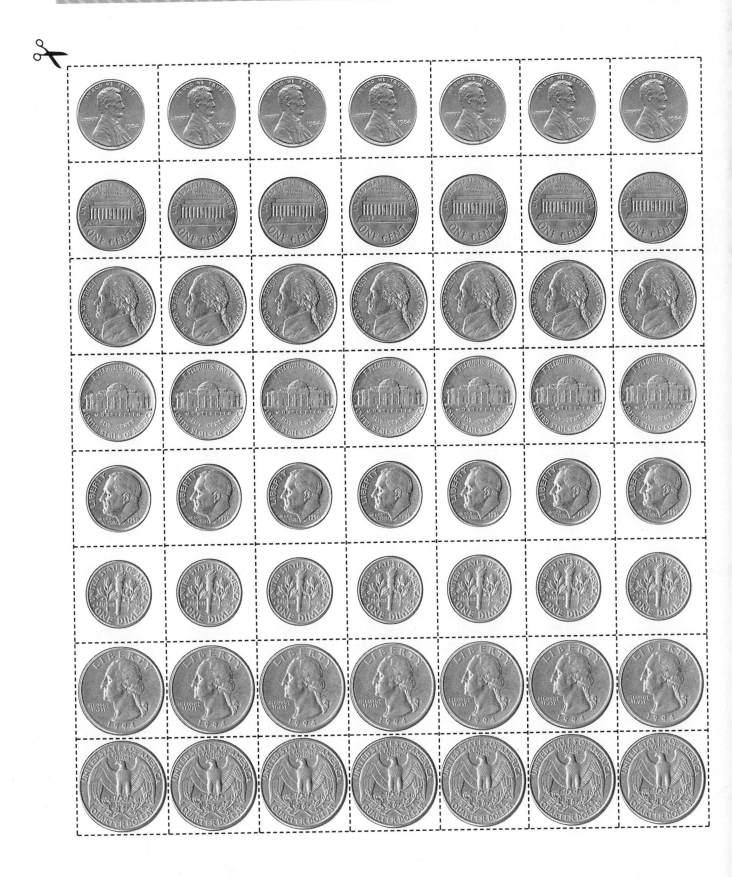

Use with activity on page 40.

Use with activity on page 47.

Activity Sheet 2

Activity
Sheet
3

0

4

1

5

2

6

3

7

8

12

9

13

10

14

11

15

Use with activities on pages 50 and 278.

Activity Sheet 4

Symmetry in Geometry Shapes

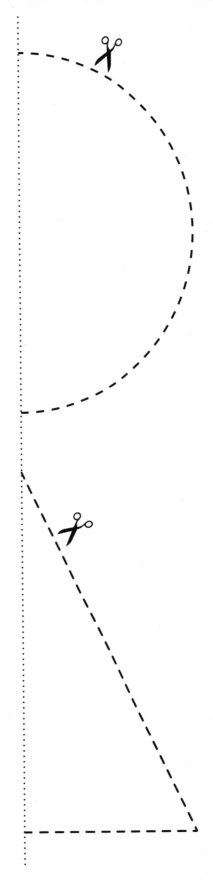

Symmetry for Winter: Snowflake

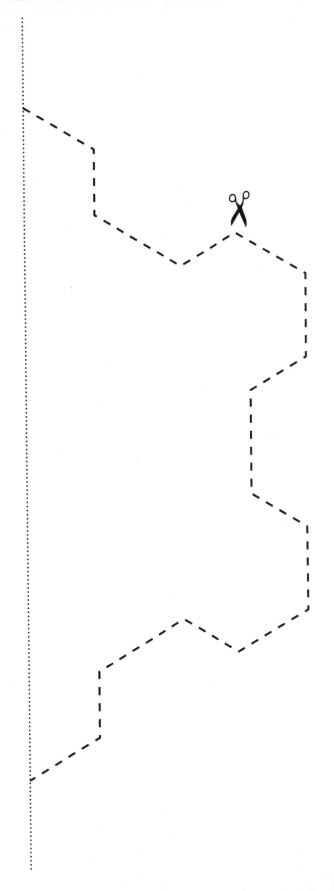

Use with activity on page 65.

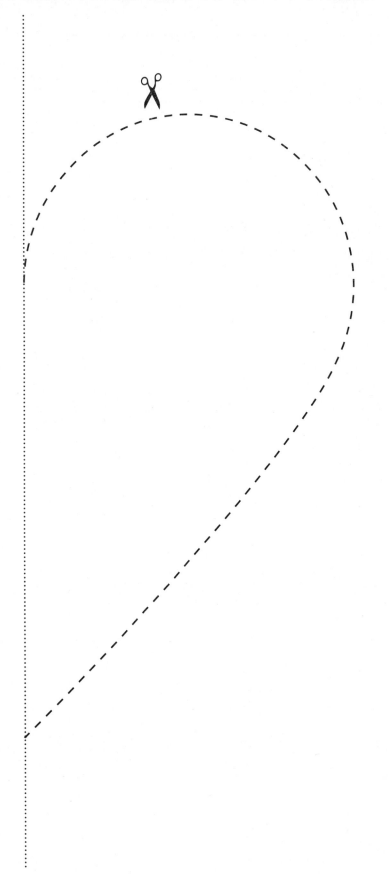

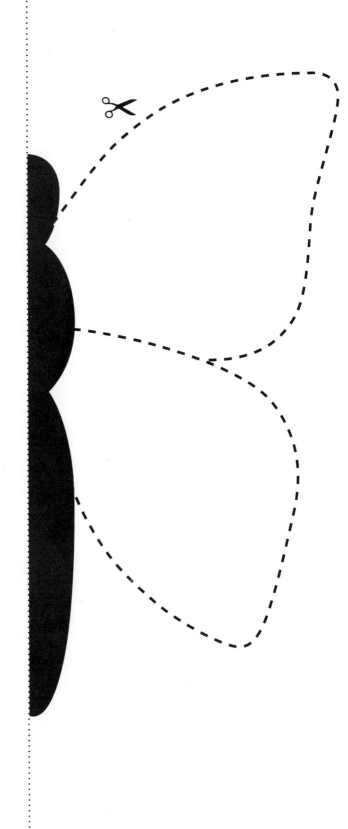

Name: _____

Telephone Number: **1 –** _____ **–** _____ **–** _____
                          (area code)

Spin a Number (1–10) Game Mat

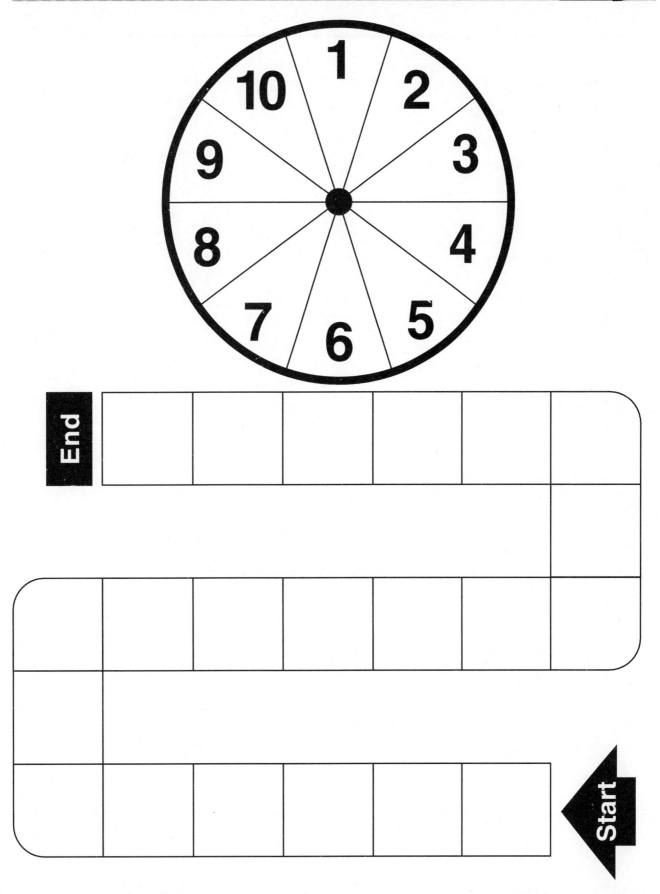

Activity Sheet 10

Use with activity on page 84.

Use with activity on page 84.

Activity Sheet 12

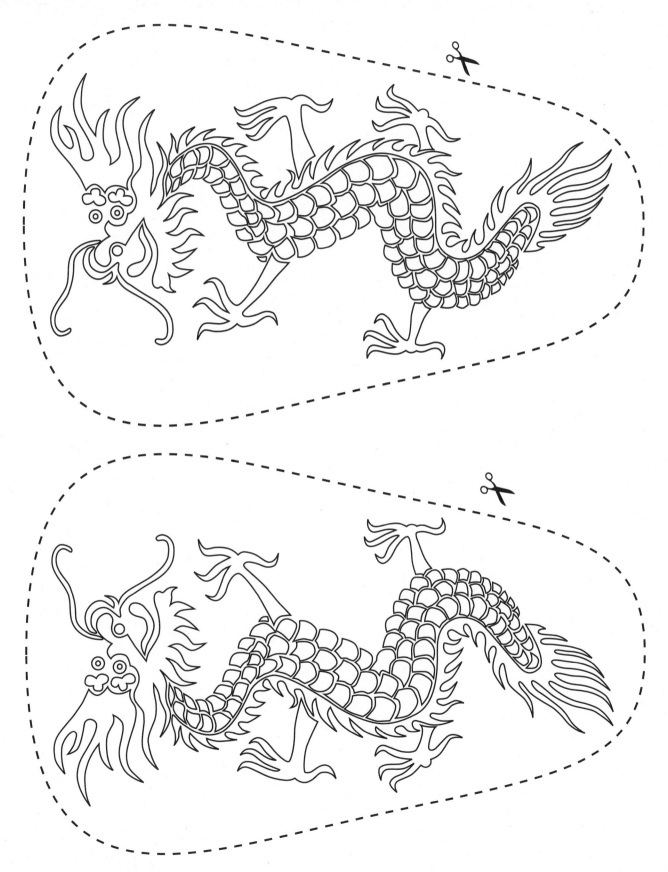

Use with activity on page 86.

Activity Sheet 13

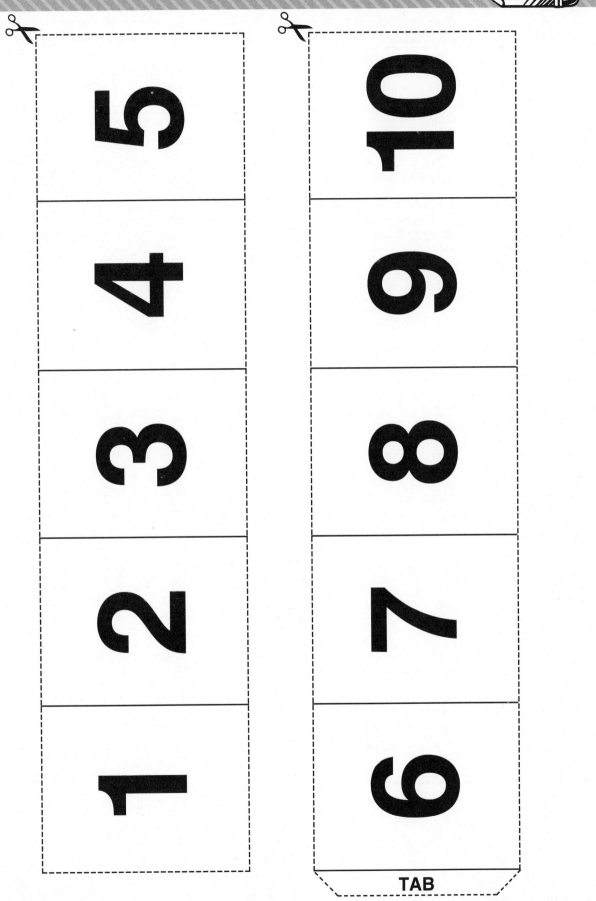

5

4

3

2

1

10

9

8

7

6

TAB

Use with activity on page 86.

Activity Sheet 14

TAB

TAB

Use with activity on page 86.

Activity Sheet 15

is taller.

is about
the same.

is shorter.

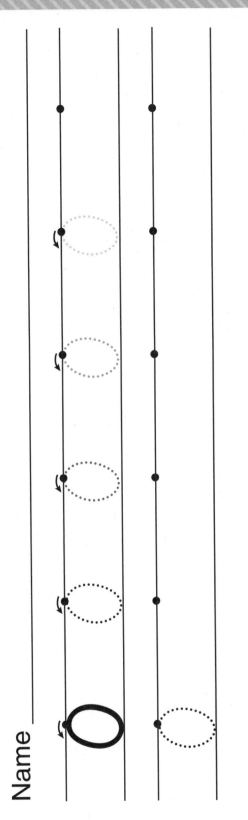

Name

Name

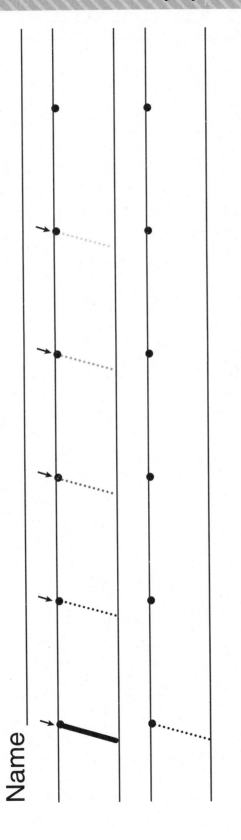

Number Book (2)

Name

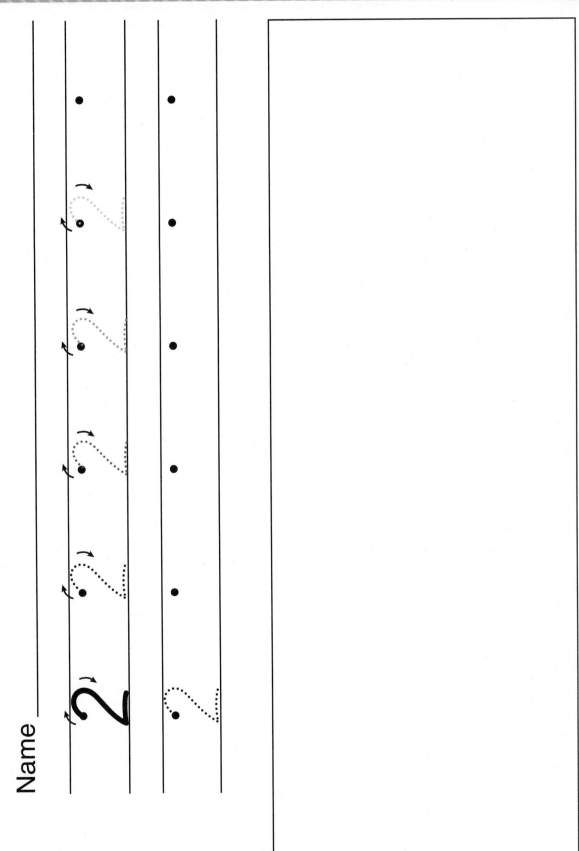

Number Book (3)

Name

3

Number Book (4)

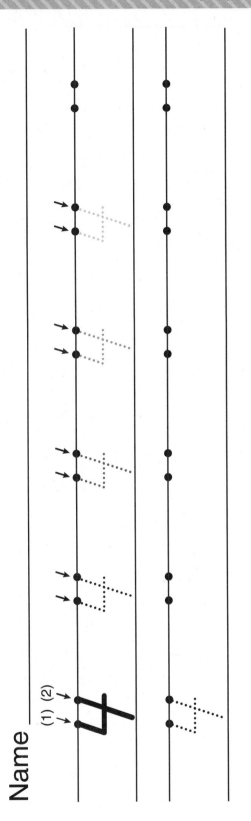

Name

(1) (2)

Use with activity on page 112.

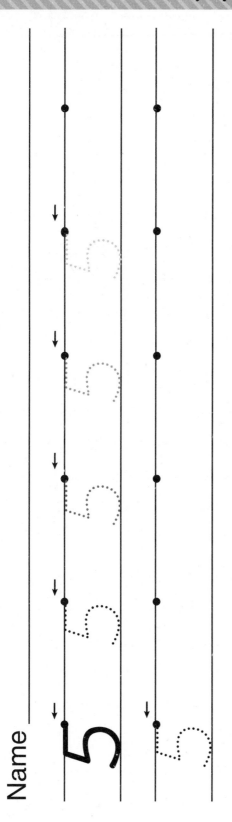

Name

5

Number Book (6)

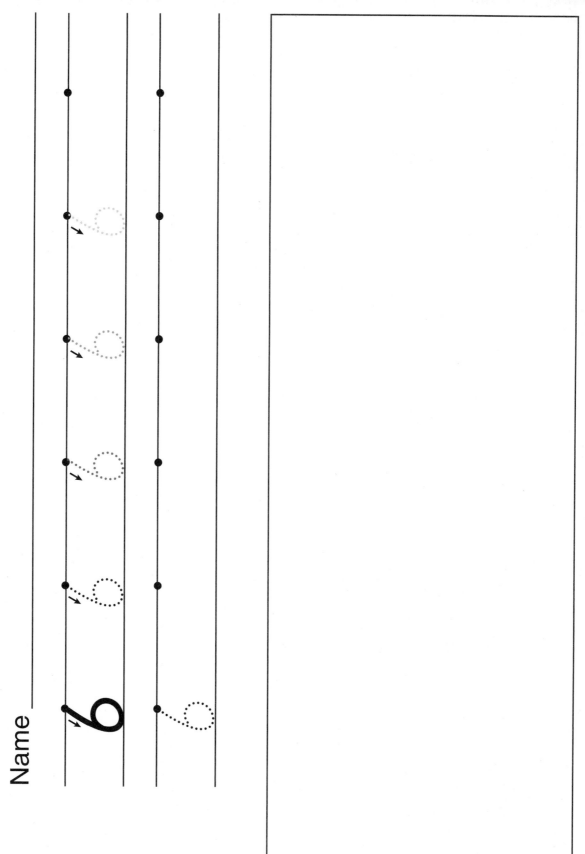

Name

Name

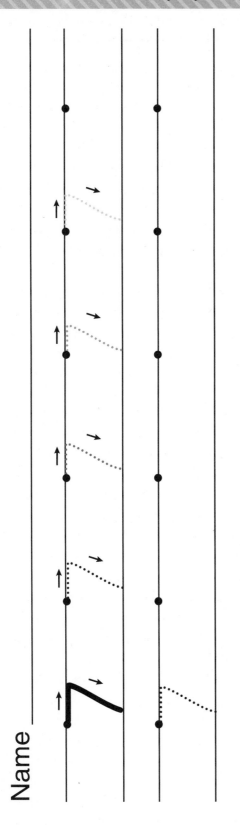

Use with activity on page 112.

Activity Sheet 24

Name

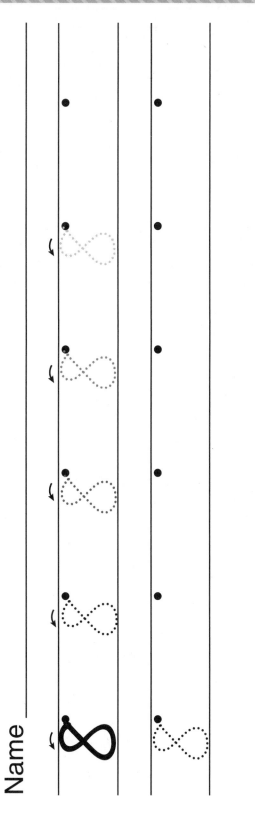

Name

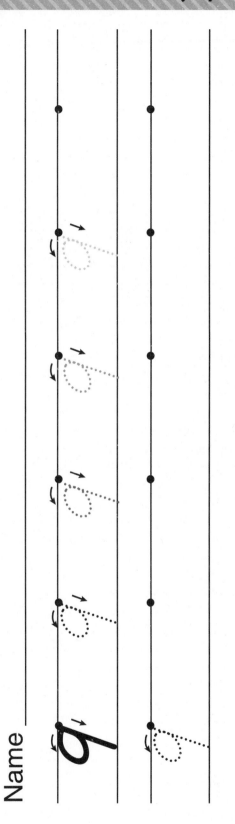

Name

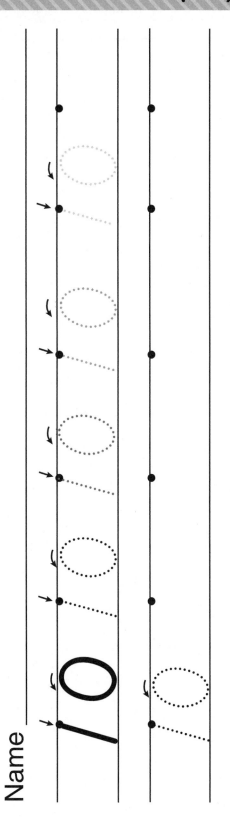

Number Book (blank)

Name

Activity Sheet 28

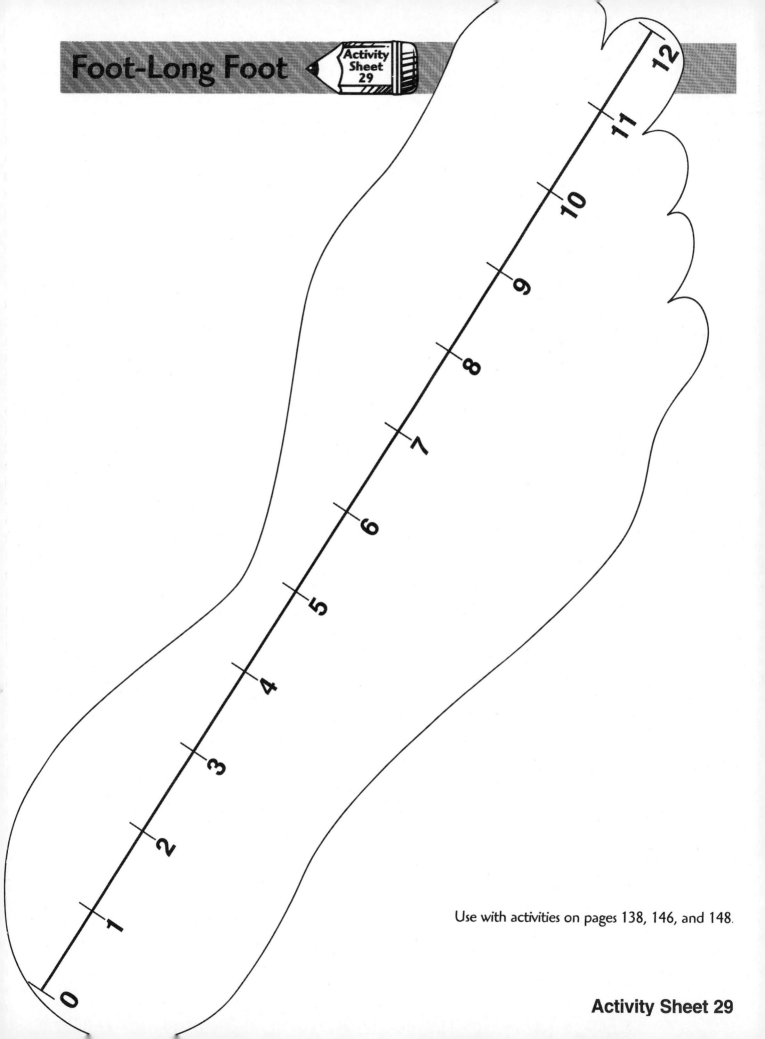

Foot-Long Foot

Use with activities on pages 138, 146, and 148.

Pattern-Block Puzzle 1

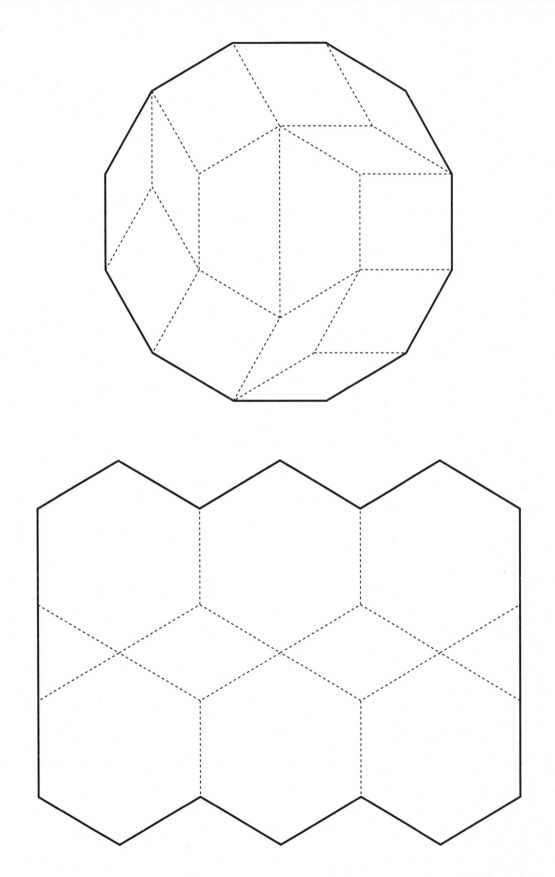

Use with activity on page 162.

Activity Sheet 30

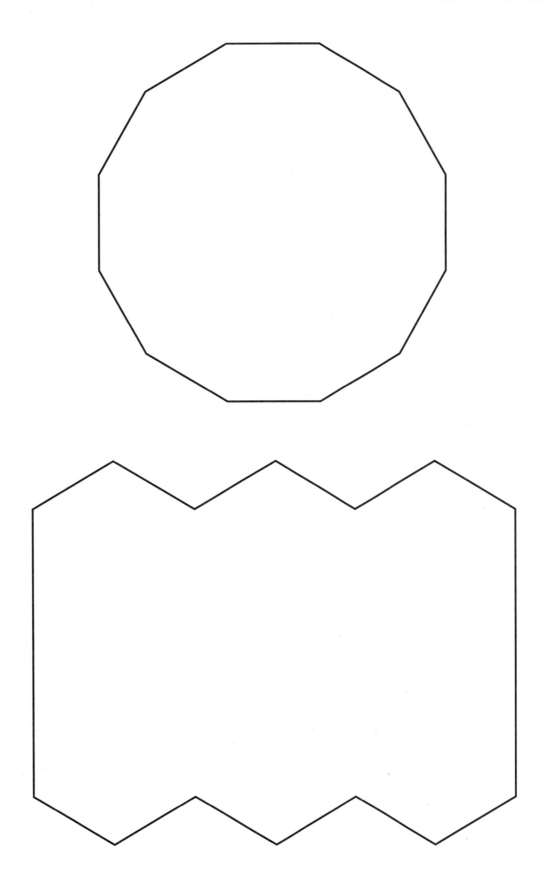

Use with activity on page 162.

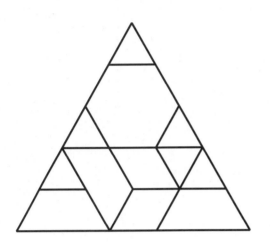

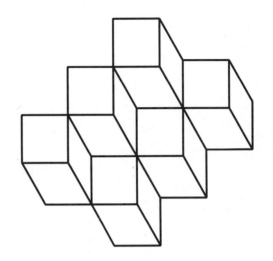

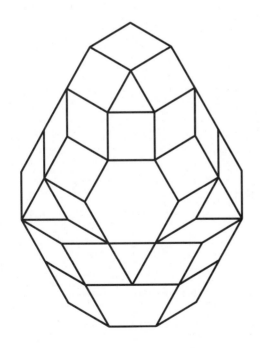

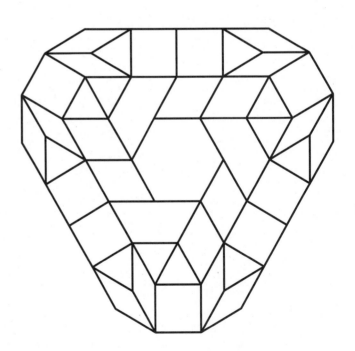

Use with activity on page 162.

Paper Clock

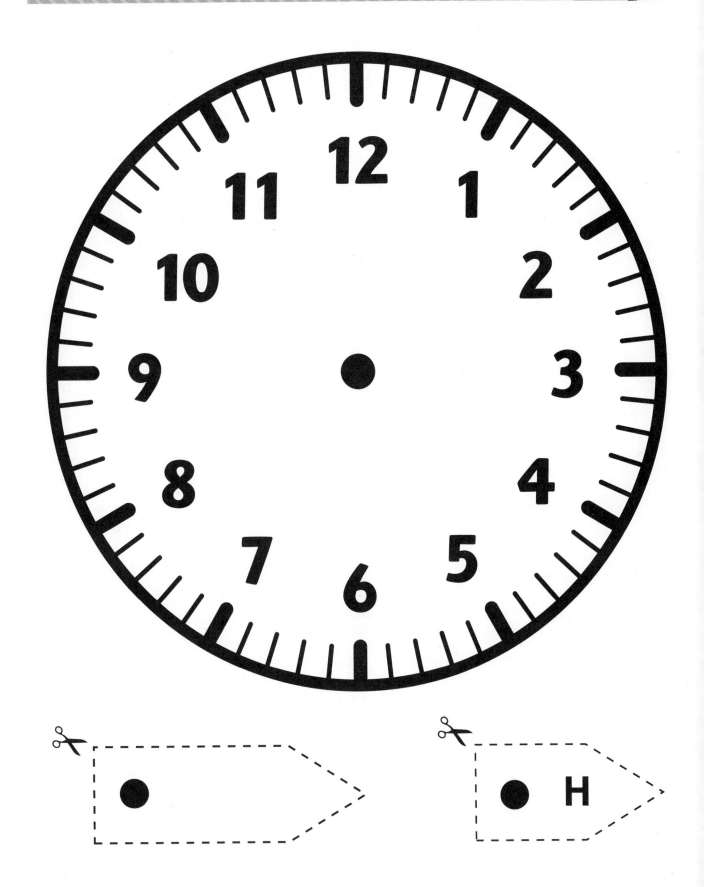

H

Number Grid

									1
									0

Use with activity on page 222.

Activity Sheet 34

Checkerboard

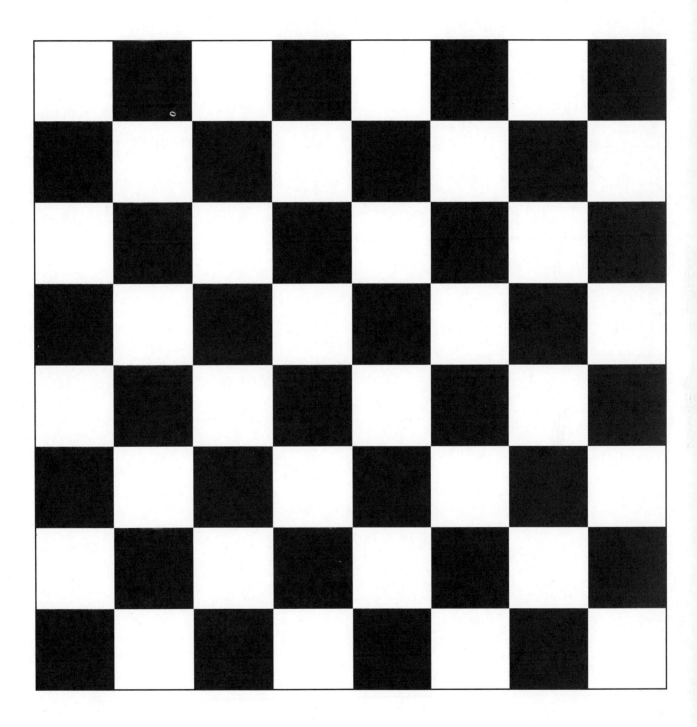

Use with activity on page 227.

Recipe for Modeling Dough

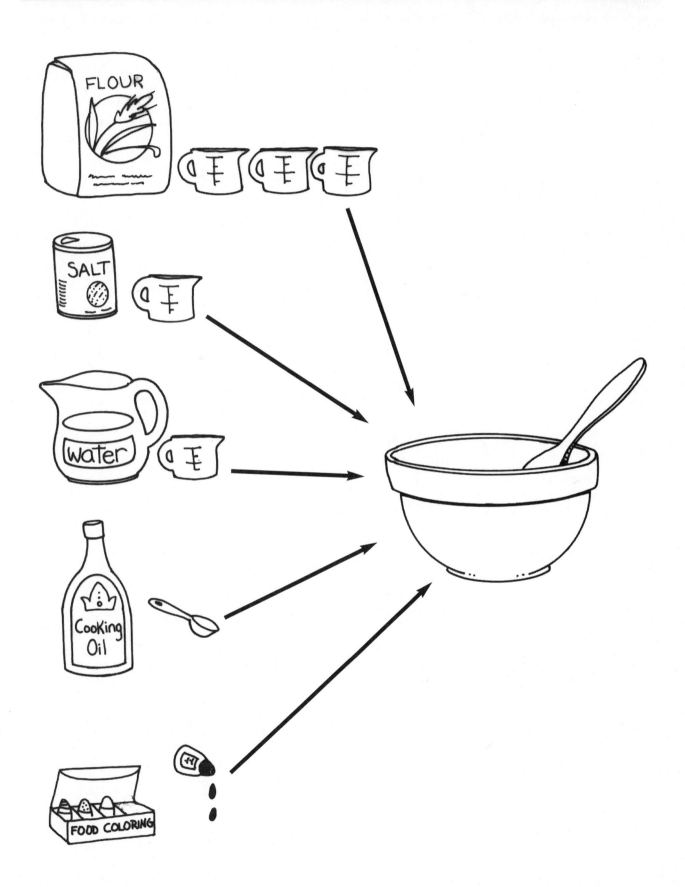

Use with activity on page 242 mod 272.

Activity Sheet 36

Use with activity on page 258.

Clock Faces (blank)

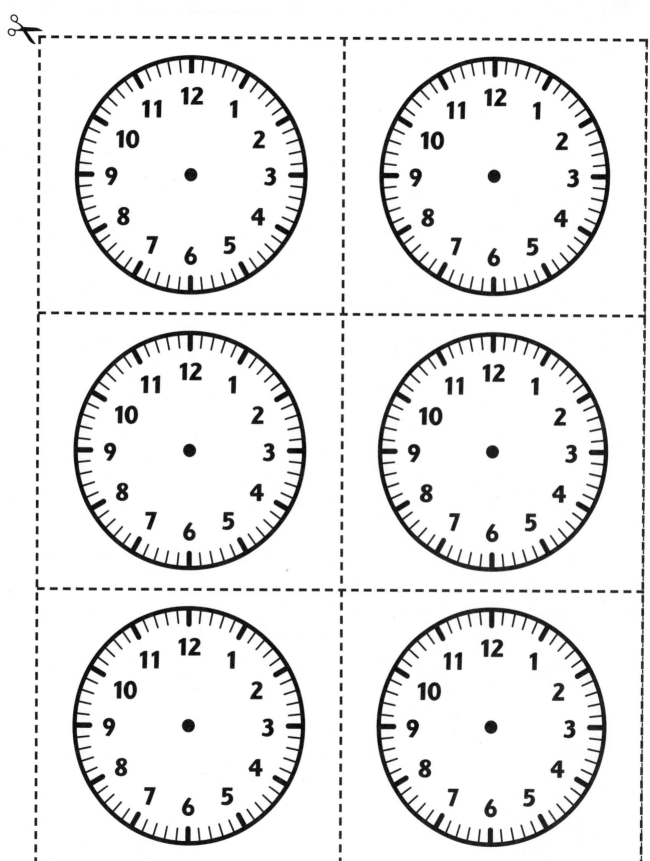

Use with activity on page 258.

Digital Clock Faces (blank)

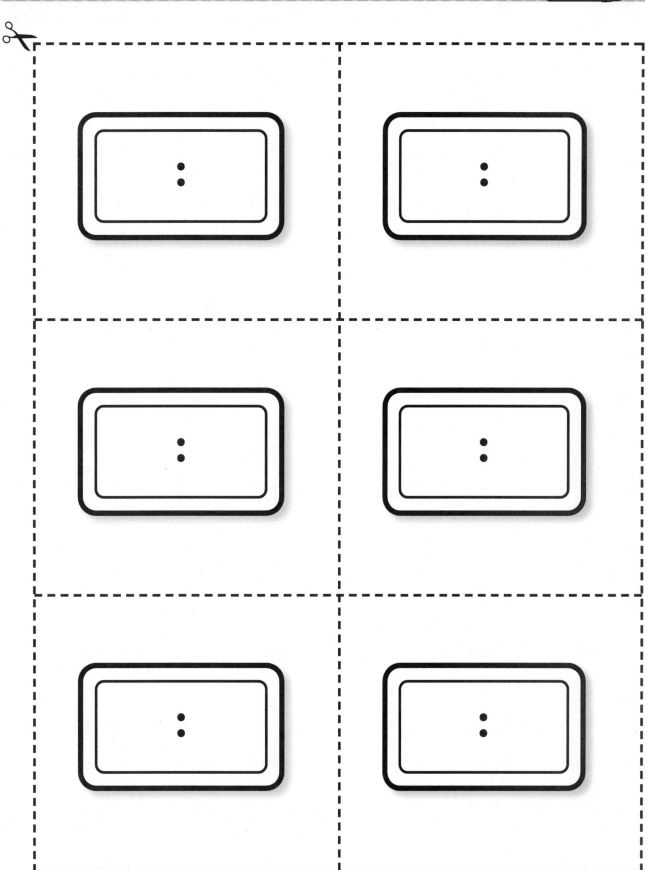

$1 Bills (fronts)

Activity Sheet 41

$1 Bills (backs)

Activity Sheet 42

Use with activities on pages 264, 266, 280, 281, 292, and 294.

Use with activities on pages 280, 281, 292, and 294.

Activity Sheet 43

$1, $10, and $100 Bills (backs)

Use with activities on pages 280, 281, 292, and 294.

Dice Throw Grid

2								
3								
4								
5								
6								
7								
8								
9								
10								
11								
12								

Use with activitiy on page 296.

Activity Sheet 45

Home Links

Home Links (cont.)

A Letter to Parents about Home Links

When children are read to, they learn to love books and want to become readers themselves. In the same way, children develop positive feelings about mathematics by sharing pleasurable experiences as they count, measure, compare, estimate, and discover patterns in everyday life.

Kindergarten Home Links provide a guide to a variety of activities that parents and children can share in a spirit of exploration and enjoyment, much as they share interesting stories.

The reward for young children is that mathematics will not become a puzzling abstraction, but will make sense to them as part of their real world.

Family Note

Keep in mind that children enjoy counting things. Be on the lookout for opportunities to practice this skill. You'll be pleasantly surprised how counting things brings about many playful and productive mathematics activities. Counting hops, skips, jumps, and side-steps helps children develop counting skills, as well as coordination.

Count the steps you need to walk from the sidewalk to the front door (or any two places). Try to walk the same distance with fewer steps or with more steps.

Get into the counting habit!

When you take a walk, try hopping, skipping, jumping, or side-stepping a certain number of times.

Family Note

As you do this and other counting activities, remember, of course, not to overdo it—avoid making counting a tedious activity!

Start a family penny jar to collect some of your family's pennies.

Count them once a week and watch the collection grow.

To add variety, sometimes count pennies backward after you have picked them up:

10 ... 9 ... 8 ... 7 ... 6 ... 5 ... 4 ... 3 ... 2 ... 1 ... 0

You can get better at counting backward if you practice. (Begin at 10. Later, try counting back from a higher number.)

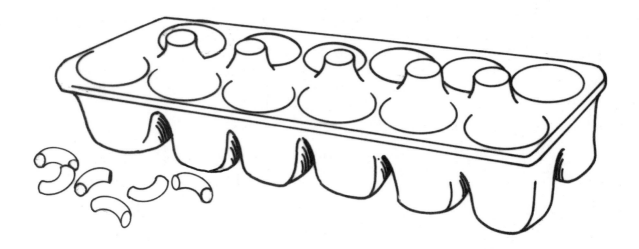

Mark each cup in an empty egg carton with the numbers 1 through 12.

Count out the right number of an item for each cup. Try uncooked macaroni or beans.

Guess how many pieces you put in all the cups together.

Count them to see how close you were.

Order in Counting

Family Note

In this activity, children count objects using such words as *first, second,* and *third* to describe the order of the objects. Look for opportunities to use these words. For example, you may have a child in *third* grade; school classes are arranged in order. When you are waiting together in a line, explain that you are *third* in line or *second* in line. Dates are referred to by order; for example, October *second* or January *eighth*.

Line up five or more favorite toys.

Which one is first? Second? Fifth?
Count them in order: first, second, third, and so on.

Put the toys in a different order.
Now which one is first? Second? Fifth?

Line up more than five things.
Can you count these in order?

Family Note

Look for natural ways to make mathematics vocabulary a part of everyday language. Use such words as *closer/farther, more/less, short/shorter/shortest, above/below,* and *inside/outside* to help give meaning to these terms. Then, those words become familiar and comfortable for children to use.

Look around a room.
Find five things that are above an object.

Example: The ceiling is *above* the floor.

Find five things that are below an object.

Example: The rug is *below* the table.

Treasure Hunt

Family Note

In this activity, children become more comfortable with mathematics language, including attributes. You may find it helpful to keep the following definition in mind.

Attributes: When you describe an object by its physical characteristics, such as size, color, thickness, you are describing it by its attributes.

Have a treasure hunt.

▷ Find a small ball and a large ball.

▷ Find a little pillow and a big pillow.

▷ Find a thin book and a thick book.

▷ Find something taller than you and something shorter than you.

Family Note

As children begin to look for measurements, they will find many ways to explore different kinds of measurements in natural settings. When they use words that compare the sizes and weights of things, how far away or how close they are, or how much more of something you need, they are using math ideas. It's helpful to get children in the habit of using these terms.

Compare the weight of two objects by holding one in each hand.

Can you tell which is heavier? Lighter?

How might you compare the weights of three different objects?

Family Note

The concept of passing time can be difficult for young children to understand. Talking about how many minutes or hours it takes to do something or go somewhere and using clocks and calendars will help your child begin to grasp this concept. Children can learn a great deal from using these timing devices, and they enjoy doing it.

Set the kitchen timer when you are cooking.

Think of other ways that setting a timer might be useful. For example, estimate how long it will take to get dressed. Set the timer, and then try to beat it.

Mark the Calendar

Family Note

Think of your home as a rich source of time-telling devices. Children can learn a lot by setting alarm clocks, as well as watching microwave oven countdowns and digital clock displays. All these experiences can provide valuable lessons for developing a sense of time.

Use a calendar to keep track of time and to mark special days.

It's easy to forget the date library books are due. Keep track! Check the due date. Mark it on the calendar.

Family Note

As children become more aware of time and clocks, help them make connections between time and activities that they enjoy. For example, sometimes when children are going to watch a favorite TV show, let them be responsible for turning the television on at the correct time. Explain where the hour and minute hands will be on the clock. Drawing a picture or setting the hands of a play clock for the correct time can be helpful.

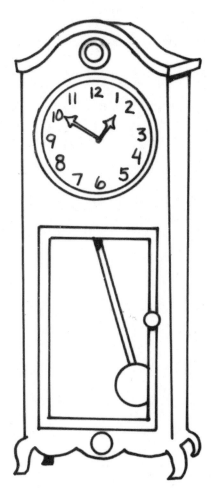

Try being a "person timer." Saying "one thousand" before each number you count is like timing in seconds. For example, "One thousand one, one thousand two" will take about two seconds to say.

Try to guess how long a minute lasts. Clap your hands when you think a minute has passed. Check the clock to see how close you were.

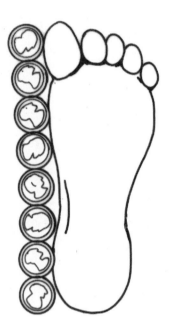

Estimate the length of a shoe, a pencil, or a floor tile in "penny lengths" instead of inches. Then use pennies to measure the "penny length." Was your estimate close?

A penny is about 2 centimeters or $\frac{3}{4}$ of an inch in diameter.

Family Note

Remember to encourage your child to make guesses about numbers of objects in everyday situations and then try to count the objects if possible. For example, at the grocery store, estimate how many items you have in the grocery cart and then count them together as you put the items through the checkout lane.

Pick up a small handful of raisins or nuts and guess how many there are in the pile.

Guess how many raisins are in a mini-box, how many chips are in a cookie, or how many grapes are in a small bunch. Then count as you eat each piece of food.

Guess how many wheels are in your home. Don't forget wheels on cars, bicycles, toys, and vacuum cleaners. Count to see how many wheels there really are. Try using tally marks while you count.

Tally Marks

/ (one)

// (two)

/// (three)

//// (four)

⧸⧸⧸⧸⧸ (five)

⧸⧸⧸⧸⧸ /// (eight)

Bring a report to school of the number of wheels there are in your home.

Play "I Spy" with someone. Pick an object that you can see. Give a clue about the shape of the object. The other person guesses which object you are describing. Begin with easy clues and then give some harder ones.

For example

▷ "I spy something that is round."

▷ "I spy something that is round and has two hands."

▷ "I spy something that is a rectangle and has rectangular buttons."

Take turns trying to stump each other.

Family Note

The recipe below provides a valuable opportunity to explore geometric shapes and is also an excellent measurement activity!

Eat a geometric treat.

Make a peanut butter sandwich (or some other favorite). Cut it in half. Try to nibble one half into a circle and the other half into a square, a triangle, or a different shape.

Peanut Butter Balls (makes about ten 1-inch balls)

1. Mix about $\frac{3}{4}$ cup of crunchy peanut butter with $1\frac{1}{2}$ tbsp of honey or sugar. (These are nicer if they aren't too sweet.)

2. Gradually, add $1\frac{1}{8}$ cups (depends on the thickness of the peanut butter) powdered skim milk to make a dough stiff enough to roll into balls.

3. Make some big, some small, and some equal-size balls.

4. Try some other shapes: ovals, cylinders, and so on.

5. If you want, coat the shapes with sesame seeds.

6. Chill, then eat. Yummy!

Family Note

Keep in mind that children need to talk about their ideas and to have someone listen. Encourage children to discuss reasons why you or they make certain decisions. Be accepting instead of critical—it is the habit of discussion which is most valuable. Help your child become a good problem solver. Look for opportunities to figure out answers to real-life questions.

We have to go to the library, the grocery store, the park, and the post office today.

Where should we go first?

Where should we go last?

We have one can of tuna, and we need five.
How many more do we need to buy?

Family Note

Take advantage of the opportunities for math talk while taking a trip in the car. Before or during a car trip, discuss the following questions:
  ▷ What route will we take to get to our destination?
  ▷ About how far will we travel?
  ▷ How long it will take to get to our destination?

Look at the gauges on the dashboard. What information can you discover from them?

As the gauges become familiar, talk about questions like this:

  ▷ About how much gas is left?

Before starting a trip, make sure that the trip meter is set at 0.

  ▷ How many miles are there on the trip meter as we start a journey? (Zero!)

  ▷ About how many miles are on the trip meter at the end of the journey? (Ignore the tenths of a mile.)

A harder question is:

  ▷ How many miles are on the odometer?

Take a walk around your house looking for numbers.

Where did you find the most? In your bedroom? In the kitchen?

Where else did you find numbers?

Draw a picture of some of the things with numbers that you found.

Family Note

Remember to look around for patterns with children. Patterns are everywhere—in music, nature, language, and art. The more you become aware of their presence, the more you'll find.

Play some music and listen to the beat. Clap to the beat that you hear.

Can you clap and tap your foot to the beat at the same time?

How else can you copy the pattern?

Listen to a pattern and then repeat it.

Clap! Clap! Snap!
Clap! Clap! Snap!

Take turns making patterns using your feet, your hands, and other sounds.

> **Family Note**
>
> With your child, find patterns around your house and neighborhood. Look at fences, buildings, doors, windows, wallpaper, and fabrics. Try to draw some patterns that you see together. You may be able to take a camera along and record some patterns you find.

Look for outdoor objects that have patterns or geometric shapes on them.

Take a look at the leaves on different trees.

What do you notice about their size, shape, edges, and veins?

How are they the same? How are they different?

Look at patterns in spider webs.
Find shapes in the webs.

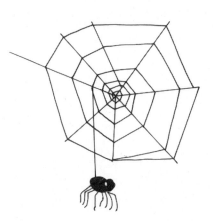

Family Note

Good rote counting skills help children become aware of the patterns and the structure of our number system.

In addition to counting actual objects, children enjoy the rhythm and pattern of reciting numbers in order, or rote counting. Encourage them to count as far as they can. From time to time, help them go a little further. Children gain a real sense of power when they are able to reach 100.

Practice counting to 100.

First, start counting at 1. Then start at other numbers: 15, 27, 45 ... .

Count backward sometimes. Rocket liftoffs, timers, and microwaves count down to 0.
Try starting from the teens or higher numbers too: 13, 12, 11 ... .

Family Note

Counts by numbers other than 1 not only help counting efficiency but help children develop number patterns which are beneficial in later grades.

Counting by 2s.

Look for things around the house that come in pairs (socks, shoes, mittens, and boots, for example). You can count the pairs by 2s.

Counting by 5s.

Count the fingers in your family. Count by 5s. How about toes?

Begin a nickel collection. Keep adding to it. Once in a while count how much money is in your nickel collection. Count by 5s.

Family Note

Sorting helps children develop the ability to examine a variety of items and to develop classification categories into which they can be grouped.

Before unpacking a grocery bag, take a moment to guess about how many items are inside the bag. Then count to see how close you were.

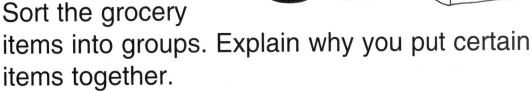

Sort the grocery items into groups. Explain why you put certain items together.

Can you think of a different way to sort the items?

Family Note

As you compare numbers of seeds in apples and numbers of sections in oranges, encourage your child to use mathematical terms like *more, less, about the same,* and *equal.*

Do all apples have the same number of seeds? About how many do you think they have? Take a guess.

Keep track as your family eats some apples over a few days and find out.

How about sections of an orange? Do all oranges have the same number of sections?

Family Note

As children learn more about different types of measurement, they will also be learning the vocabulary of measurement. To strengthen this vocabulary, use measurement language in conversations with your child. When speaking of distances, try to use relative terms such as *farther, nearer, closer* that help to make comparisons. For example: *Which is nearer, your school or the grocery store? Which is farther away, the brown sofa or the blue lamp?*

Record family heights by marking them on a door frame. You can record heights in centimeters and in inches. The centimeter number will be larger even though the height is the same. Why?

Measure again in the same place several months later.

Have the measurements changed?

Weighing Apples

 Family Note

Keep in mind that it is important for young children to see and informally use different kinds of measures and measuring tools, such as rulers, timers, measuring cups and spoons, and scales in their everyday lives.

You'll find lots of mathematics at the grocery store.

Choose several apples in the produce section and estimate about how much they weigh. Then weigh them to check how close your estimate is.

>
> ***Family Note***
>
> For this activity, make sure that the containers are nonbreakable. Bath time provides an excellent opportunity to experiment and play with these containers.
>
> The process of filling containers and comparing how much each can hold gives children the opportunity to experiment with the measurement of volume without worrying about exact answers.

Collect some containers that are different shapes and sizes, such as cottage cheese cartons, plastic bottles, and juice containers.

Use the containers to pour water back and forth. Try to find out which container holds the most, which holds the least, and which containers hold about the same amount.

Family Note

Remember to take advantage of all the opportunities for mathematics learning that are a part of making meals and snacks with your child. In this activity, use the terms *thick, thicker, thickest, thin, thinner,* and *thinnest* when comparing the bread to the filling in a sandwich.

Make a favorite sandwich.

Compare the bread to the filling.

Cut the sandwich in half.

Then cut the halves into quarters.

Use fraction names to describe the parts as someone cuts them.

Are fourths of the sandwich larger or smaller than halves?

Have someone cut an apple for you. Say whether you want it cut in halves, quarters, or eighths.

Watch as the apple is cut into those parts. Are the pieces equal in size?

Family Note

In this activity, children compare two books. Be on the lookout for things you can compare using some of these words:

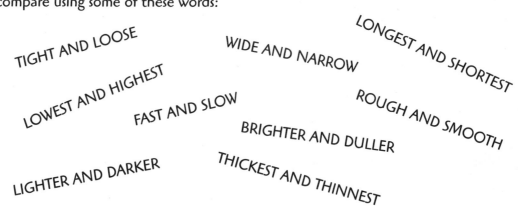

TIGHT AND LOOSE

LOWEST AND HIGHEST

FAST AND SLOW

LIGHTER AND DARKER

WIDE AND NARROW

BRIGHTER AND DULLER

THICKEST AND THINNEST

LONGEST AND SHORTEST

ROUGH AND SMOOTH

Most and *least* are useful terms to understand.

Compare two books.

Which one has more pages?

Which one has fewer pages?

How did you find the number of pages?

Did you estimate, count, or look at the last page number?

Family Note

The word *pattern* has many different meanings. Here, pattern is defined as a simple arrangement of objects, such that one can tell what will come next if the arrangement is continued. The concept of predictable patterns is an important part of mathematics.

To dye pasta for color patterns in this activity, place the pasta in a jar with some rubbing alcohol and a few drops of food coloring. Shake the jar and then lay the pasta on a sheet of newspaper to dry. Or you can buy pasta in different colors in many grocery stores.

You can make patterns with food. Make some patterns with cereals and crackers that have different shapes and colors. If the cereal has holes, string a cereal pattern on yarn to make a necklace or bracelet that you can eat.

Or

Make patterns with different kinds of tube-shaped pasta. Use plain or colored pasta. Sort by color, shape, or both. Make your patterns into necklaces or bracelets or glue them on paper. (Do not eat these patterns!)

Family Note

Many children know the meaning of some signs and signals before they can read. For example, they may know that it is safe to walk across the street when there is a green light, but they may not recognize additional signs with different shapes and colors.

As you talk about signs, use the terms *circle, octagon, diamond* (or *rhombus*), and *rectangle* to describe the shapes. In addition to learning the names of the shapes, your child will become an observant traveler.

Look at the different shapes of road signs and safety signs. What shapes do you see? Why are stop signs, caution signs, and information signs shaped differently?

Family Note

Collecting data helps children sort, record, count, compare, and visualize complex information.

What do you think is the most popular car color?

Make a guess. Then, when you are on a trip or in a parking lot, check your answer.

What did you find out?

Family Note

On Home Link 2, Collecting Pennies, you began to collect pennies in a family penny jar. By this point in the year, you will probably have a large number of pennies in the jar. This collection can be an excellent tool for many counting and estimation activities.

Try counting the pennies in your family penny jar for a really big count. Can you think of a good way to help keep track of the total?

Make piles of ten and count by tens.

Counting Past 100

Family Note

Try counting backward. This is good practice for becoming a nimble counter. Try starting from different numbers. A common counting pitfall often occurs when children reach the 100 number barrier. Instead of counting "101, 102, 103," and so on, they begin to count by hundreds: "100, 200, 300" and so on.

Practice counting past 100. Start from different numbers, such as 81, 92, and 68.

Practice counting by 2s, 5s, or 10s.
This is called "skip counting."

Family Note

You may want to repeat this activity from time to time to see if there is much weight change over time. Once in a while, try estimating weights of other things. Weigh them and check the weights against your estimates.

Guess how much you weigh. Weigh yourself on a scale to check your estimate.

A young beaver weighs about 40 pounds. Do you weigh more or less than a young beaver?

Try to assemble a pile of objects on a bath scale that weighs about the same amount as you.

Family Note

Pizzas offer a good chance to talk about shapes and fractions. Take the opportunity to talk about fractions as you cut other foods, such as sandwiches, cakes, and bread into equal parts.

Watch someone cut a pizza into equal pieces. Count the pieces. Use fraction names to describe the pieces.

For example, if someone cuts a pizza into 4 pieces, each piece is $\frac{1}{4}$ of the whole pizza.

Compare the sizes of the pieces as someone divides the pizza into smaller and smaller sections. Is $\frac{1}{2}$ of the pizza smaller or larger than $\frac{1}{4}$ of the pizza?

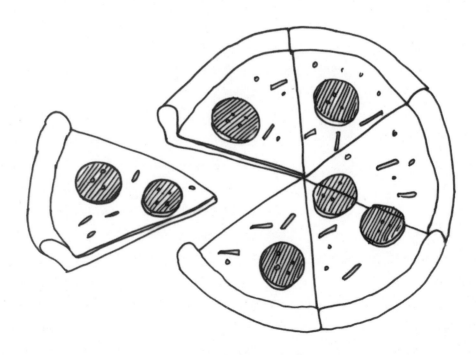

Family Note

When you do this activity, help your child find a place to keep the collection of objects. Add to the collection on a regular basis.

Collect different kinds and sizes of objects, such as: lids from juice bottles, soda bottles, and buttons.

Use the objects to make patterns.

Try to describe the pattern to someone.

Use other collections to make patterns, such as pennies, nickels, and dimes.

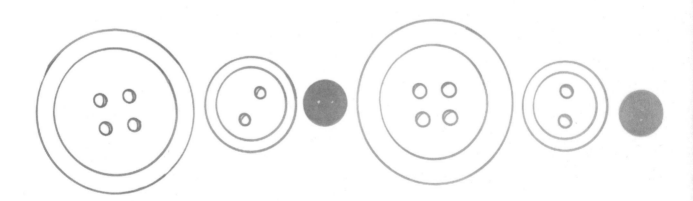

Family Note

Calendars offer many valuable opportunities for children to count and read numbers. Talk about extending your Kindergartener's personal calendar into a family calendar on which you can record important family appointments, events, and occasions.

Look at your calendar to find answers to the following questions:

▷ How many days are there this month?

▷ How many Wednesdays? Fridays? Sundays?

▷ What day is the first? The fifth?

▷ What is today's date?

▷ How many days are left in this month?

▷ Mark special days like birthdays and holidays.

Family Note

As children learn about time, they may have difficulty at first understanding how long a minute is. In this activity, children think about what they are able to do in a minute or in multi-minute intervals. You may want to occasionally extend this to timing other activities or chores.

Think of three things you can do in one minute or less.

Have someone time you to see if you really can do all three things in a minute.

For example, can you touch your toes ten times, do five jumping jacks, and spin around three times in one minute?

Guess how much of your room you can clean in two minutes and then try cleaning it for two minutes.

Did you do more or less than you thought you would?

Was your prediction close, or were you surprised at the result?

Family Note

Most likely you have many thermometers in your home. Look around together with your child and make a list of the thermometers you have. For example you might find an oven thermometer, a refrigerator thermometer, a people thermometer, a meat thermometer, or a candy thermometer. Keep a lookout in your neighborhood for other thermometers.

Listen to the weather report on television or radio. Compare the temperature given to the reading on your own home thermometer. Are they the same or different?

Check the thermometer at the same time of day for a few days in a row.

Has the temperature stayed the same? Is it higher or lower? You might want to record the temperature on your calendar.

Before reading the thermometer, predict whether today is warmer or colder than yesterday. Then check to see if you were right.

Family Note

Encourage discussion about the shape you build in this activity. Ask such questions as:

▷ Which shape used the most marshmallows or gumdrops?

▷ Do any shapes have more toothpicks than marshmallows?

▷ How many triangles did you make? How many rectangles?

▷ Which structure keeps its shape the best?

Build shapes and structures with miniature marshmallows or gumdrops and toothpicks.

Begin with flat 2-dimensional shapes, then try building up to 3-dimensional shapes, such as cubes, pyramids, and prisms.

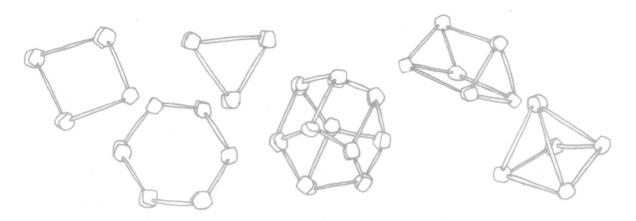

Bring one or two of your shapes to school.

Shape Snack

Plan and prepare a shape snack with someone.

▷ Cut cheese into squares and triangles.

▷ Choose crackers that are squares and circles.

▷ Grapes are spheres.

▷ Slice oranges into circles.

▷ For a cylinder, try a glass of milk.

Grocery Store Mathematics

Family Note

Keep the following definition in mind as you do this activity.

Array: *a rectangular arrangement of objects in rows and columns.*

Later on, arrays will play an important role in demonstrating multiplication.

Grocery stores are a gold mine for mathematics. There are lots of numbers, shapes, arrangements, measures, and problems to be solved.

Look for different shapes: cylinder, rectangular prism (such as a cereal box), pyramid, sphere, circle, oval, square, rectangle, and triangle.

Look for products packaged in regular arrangements of arrays, such as eggs (a 2 × 6 or 3 × 4 array) or a six-pack of juices (a 2 × 3 array).

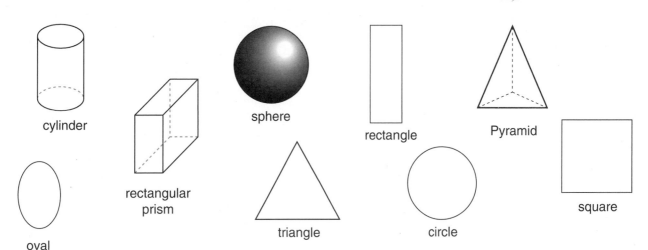

cylinder

rectangular prism

oval

sphere

triangle

rectangle

circle

Pyramid

square

Family Note

Children's earliest exposure to mathematical division is usually through "equal sharing," or dividing any whole object or group of objects into two or more equal parts or equal groups. Look for opportunities to divide objects or groups of objects into equal parts or groups.

Children understand that dividing something "equally" is the fairest way to share a treat.

Take a small group of objects, such as pennies, beans, or popcorn, and divide it into two equal groups, three equal groups, or more.

What can you do with the leftover objects?